SNOW AND PEOPLE

NIKKI BUNDEY

A ZOË BOOK

A ZOë BOOK

© 2000 Zoë Books Limited

Devised and produced by
Zoë Books Limited
15 Worthy Lane
Winchester
Hampshire SO23 7AB
England

First published in Great Britain in 2000 by
Zoë Books Limited
15 Worthy Lane
Winchester
Hampshire SO23 7AB

A record of the CIP data is available from the British
Library.

ISBN 1 86173 029 2

Printed in Italy by Grafedit SpA
Editor: Kath Davies
Design: Sterling Associates
Illustrations: Artistic License/Pete Roberts,
    Genny Haines, Tracey Fennell
Production: Grahame Griffiths

Photographic acknowledgments
The publishers wish to acknowledge, with thanks,
the following photographic sources:

Andrey Zvoznikov 6 / T Molins 7b / Brian Moser/
Granada TV 10b / 22 Hutchison Picture Library;
Ken Graham 8t / Impact Photos; B & C Alexander
- cover (inset) right, 11, 28b / John Shaw 5t / Eric
Soder 12t / Rich Kirchner 15t / David Middleton
16 / Andy Rouse 17b / NHPA; B & C Alexander
4,14 / Michael Sewell 8b / Dave Watts 29 / Still
Pictures; 12b,19,20,26,27,28t / The Stock Market;
B Vikander - cover (background), 17t / B Gadsby -
cover (inset) left / F Lulinksi - title page / J Ellard
5b / R.C.Fournier 7t / Viesti Collection 10t / N
Price 15b / D Houghton 18 / M Shirley 21t / F
Torrance 21b / M Watson 23 / J & J Wood 24t / G
Lawrence 24b / Steve Ross 25 / TRIP.

The publishers have made every effort to trace the
copyright holders, but if they have inadvertently
overlooked any, they will be pleased to make the
necessary arrangement at the first opportunity.

CONTENTS

All the words that appear in **bold** type are explained in Words we use on page 30.

WHEN IT SNOWS

When it snows, **snowflakes** float down, covering the ground in a thick white blanket. Wind can shape the **snow** into deep piles or **drifts**. Sometimes high winds blow the snow into a **blizzard**.

Water can exist in different forms. Snow is water which has frozen in the form of ice **crystals**. Water can also be a **gas**, called **water vapour**. This gas is part of the air we breathe.

Children have fun in the snow when it **settles**. They throw it at each other, make footprints in the snow and slip and slide. Adults often find snow a nuisance.

Ice crystals have frozen together to make this beautiful snowflake pattern. Each snowflake is different, but they are all six-sided, or hexagonal.

Water vapour rises when the Sun heats the air. High in the air, water vapour cools and **condenses**. It turns into **droplets** of **liquid** water. These droplets become raindrops or freeze into a **solid** state and fall as snow.

When snow melts, it turns back into water and drains away into streams and rivers. Rivers then flow to the sea. The Sun's warmth may then turn the water back into water vapour. This is called **evaporation**.

Some parts of the world have a snowy **climate**. There are heavy snowfalls on high mountains, such as the Austrian Alps.

STAYING ALIVE

Over many thousands of years, human beings have learned to live with ice and snow. In the past there were long **Ice Ages**, when the world became much colder. Ice and snow from the **Polar regions** covered more of the Earth than they do today.

Humans have a body **temperature** of about 37°C. We are **warm-blooded**. Our hair stops us losing heat through the head. In cold weather, hairs on our skin stand up on small 'goose bumps'. Hairs trap warm air around our bodies, making a layer of **insulation**.

Most snow falls at temperatures around **freezing point**. But high winds can make it seem much colder. During a blizzard there may be a complete **whiteout**. People can see nothing but snow, and may soon get lost.

In bright sunshine, snow gives off a dazzling glare. The glare causes snow-blindness. We have to wear sunglasses or goggles to protect our eyes.

Very cold weather can lower the body temperature to dangerous levels. This condition is called **hypothermia**.

One of the chief dangers of snow and ice comes from slipping and sliding. If our feet cannot grip the snowy ground, we may fall over and hurt ourselves.

Very cold, icy conditions can cause **frostbite**. It damages human skin.

DRESSING FOR SNOW

Snow is cold, wet and slippery. People protect their bodies from the cold by wearing extra layers of insulation. Blankets, jackets, hats, hoods, gloves and socks all trap the heat of the human body.

Windproof clothes protect the body from the wind's chill. The cloth is tightly woven and allows little air to pass through. The weave must not be too tight, or the body will become hot and sweaty.

Wrap up warm for a day in the snow. These children are wearing clothes made from wool and from **artificial fibres**. These keep in the warmth of their bodies.

The Inuit people live in the far north, where there is ice and snow for most of the year. Long ago, the Inuit learned to make clothes from the fur of the Polar bear or the Arctic fox and boots from caribou or seal skin. Today Inuit people wear modern, waterproof materials too.

Waterproof clothes protect us from the wetness of snow. They are made of materials which do not soak up or **absorb** water.

Boots with heavy treads on the soles help us to grip ice and snow. They increase the **friction** between the two surfaces. Metal spikes called crampons can be fitted to boots. They dig into very slippery surfaces and help people to walk.

woolly hat – reduces heat loss from head.

hood – shields face from wind, snow or hail.

goggles – protect the eyes against the glare of the snow.

anorak – waterproof and windproof covering, keeps in body warmth.

trousers – protect the legs and keep them warm.

leggings – keep trousers dry in deep snow and drifts.

boots – protect the feet, soles grip the snow.

crampons – give extra grip on slippery snow and ice.

BUILDINGS AND SHELTERS

Buildings and other shelters give people the best protection from the snow. The **structures** must be strong enough to stand up to the force of a blizzard.

The roof must bear the weight of heavy snow. Walls must keep snow out and keep in the warmth of the house. Warmth comes from people's bodies as well as from heating. Extra layers covering walls or roofs will give better insulation against the cold.

Swiss mountain houses are called *chalets*. They are made of wood and have big roofs to support winter falls of snow.

This type of tent is a *ger* or *yurt*. It is used in Central and Eastern Asia, where winters are very cold. The tent is made of woollen felt, pressed and soaked to make a thick mat. A framework of willow poles and ropes stands up to blizzards. A stove heats the tent.

The Inuit people of the Arctic used to live in tents in summer. In the winter they lived in houses made of turf and stone. The houses could stand up to heavy snowfalls.

When the Inuit went hunting they built shelters from blocks of frozen snow. The shelters protected people from cold winds and kept in warmth. Today, most Inuit people live in timber houses.

Many Inuit hunters know how to build with snow blocks. They cut the blocks with sloping edges. Each level leans further inwards to form a dome. A new fall of snow brings a new layer of insulation.

IS SNOW USEFUL?

It can be difficult to live in a snowy climate. Very few people live in the Arctic. Antarctica is home for only a few visiting scientists. However, snow has its uses. For example, people used frozen snow or ice to keep food fresh before there were **refrigerators**.

Melting snows from mountain slopes may form lakes. People sometimes build a **dam** across a lake. The lake is now a store, or reservoir, and provides water for homes, farms and factories.

Snow from mountain tops in Canada feeds many streams and rivers. The rivers provide breeding pools for salmon, which are a useful source of food for humans and wildlife.

Snow is an important source of water. Melting snows from the Himalayan mountains feed great rivers. The rivers flow through many hot, dry lands on their way to the sea. They provide water for drinking, for crop **irrigation** and for transport.

Melting snow is also a valuable source of **hydroelectric** power. At a **power station**, falling water plunges through pipes and drives whirling **turbines** to make electricity.

People use melting snow to power the turbines which make our electricity.

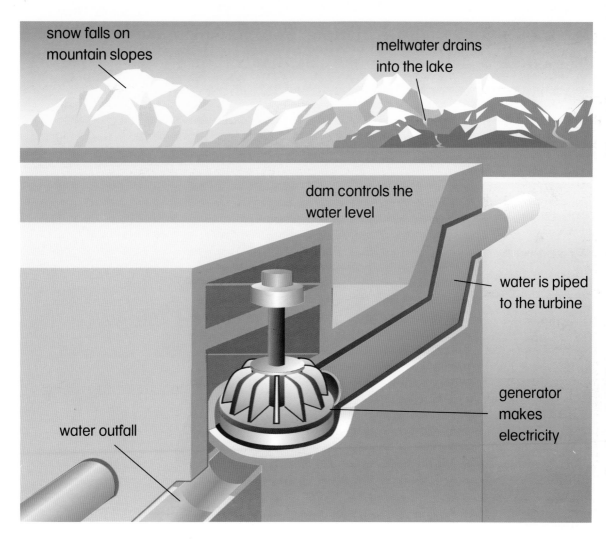

snow falls on mountain slopes

meltwater drains into the lake

dam controls the water level

water is piped to the turbine

generator makes electricity

water outfall

SNOW TRANSPORT

Snow makes travel very difficult. Drifts may block roads and railways and cut off mountain villages. We have had to find ways to make travelling over snow easier.

People have used **skis** to cross snowy countryside for at least 4,500 years. The smooth, shiny surface of the ski slides over the snow with very little friction. The runners on sleds and sleighs slide like skis. Instead of wheels, some aircraft have runners for snow landings.

Snowshoes look rather like tennis racquets. They spread the weight of the body over a larger area, so that our feet don't sink into the snow.

This large tractor is used for bringing in supplies at an Antarctic base. The metal caterpillar tracks around its wheels grip the snow. If there is enough grip to move forward, this is called **traction**.

Skiers move forwards by digging their ski sticks into the snow. Then they push or lever their bodies forwards. When skiing downhill, the force of **gravity** takes over. This tugging force pulls everything down towards the Earth. Dogs or horses sometimes pull sleighs and sleds forwards. Their feet can grip the snow.

Snow scooters or snowmobiles have runners to slide across the snow. They also have an engines for power. Wheeled tracks grip the snow to move the snowmobiles forwards.

IN THE COUNTRY

The trees of the northern forests are well designed for snow. Many trees have needles instead of leaves. They are called conifers because they have tough cones instead of flowers. Snow slides easily from their sloping branches. The weight of snow can damage smaller plants, breaking stems and twigs.

Snow blankets the fields in Colorado, USA. It protects the new shoots which will burst into leaf when spring arrives.

When snow falls on the mountains in Central Asia, herders will lead their sheep down to the shelter of the valley. They will return in spring, when the snows melt. When people and animals move according to the seasons, it is called **transhumance**.

Frost, hail and wind can damage crops. A thick layer of snow often protects new plants from frost and wind damage. Snow insulates the soil and keeps it warm.

Heavy snow can be a serious problem for hill farmers. Mountain snowdrifts may cut off flocks of sheep at the time of year when lambs are born. If snow and ice cover the ground for weeks, farmers have to take food such as hay or other fodder to the animals.

These Highland cattle can survive harsh winters in Scotland. Their long, shaggy coats keep them warm.

CITIES AND ROADS

Heavy snow can cause damage in towns and cities. It can bring down telephone lines and block streets. It can make cars **skid** on the roads and cause people to slip and fall, sometimes injuring themselves.

Snow makes it hard to clean the streets. Heated buildings make cities warm, so the snow turns into messy slush more quickly in the city than in the countryside.

This snow-plough is clearing the road. Its blade has a special shape to cut through the snow. The blade is angled so that it pushes the snow away to the side.

Car tyres have ridges called **treads**. They grip slippery road surfaces. In very bad conditions, car tyres may have chains, too. These dig into the snow and prevent skids.

People cannot use hot water to melt snow from pavements. It might re-freeze and make them even more slippery. The snow has to be cleared with a shovel. A layer of grit makes walking easier because it gives more friction and grip. Sports fields and switching systems on railways are heated to prevent them from icing over.

See for Yourself

Salt is often sprinkled on roads to keep them free from snow and ice. Salt lowers the temperature at which water freezes. Test this.
- Fill one ice-cube tray with water and place it in the freezer.

- Fill another tray with a mixture of salt and water and place it in the freezer.

- Which tray freezes first?

MOUNTAIN RESCUE

Snow storms happen very suddenly in the mountains. Paths may disappear under drifts, so safe mountain routes are often marked with high piles of rocks, called cairns. Sometimes the snow loosens and thunders down the mountainside. This is called an **avalanche**.

You must prepare carefully for a mountain walk. Check the **weather forecast** before you leave. Take a map and a **compass**. Take enough clothing to keep warm and dry. Take food and a flask of warm drink.

Power lines may be damaged during snow storms. Workers are called out to repair the damage as quickly as possible.

An injured climber is **winched** on to a helicopter. Helicopter rescue is quick, but weather conditions and steep hillsides can make flying difficult.

People must stay warm when climbing in the mountains. A light, warm blanket called a survival blanket can save your life if you are lost or injured. If you cannot move, your body will lose heat quickly. Injured climbers sometimes dig themselves a hole in the snow. The snow insulates their bodies against the wind and frost.

Mountain rescue teams try to find people who are lost in the snow. They may also rescue people after accidents such as this one. A snowmobile overturned in deep snow and people were trapped underneath it.

SNOWBALLS

Most of us do not battle with blizzards in the mountains or go on expeditions to the North Pole. We see snow in our gardens or in the local park, during the winter.

Snow is solid but it is quite soft. Air is trapped between the ice crystals. Snow is easily pressed into shapes, which is why people leave footprints in the snow and animals and birds leave tracks.

Which snowball flies faster through the air, a hard, icy one or a soft, mushy one? Which one hits a fence with the greater force, or impact?

Frozen snow is easily cut or carved. The pressure of a knife makes the snow melt slightly around the blade. This snow sculpture is in Japan.

When snow is pressed, the snowflakes crunch together tightly. The more you press a snowball with your hands, the icier it will be. It becomes harder and heavier, too, because it contains less air. Under high pressure, snow starts to melt.

Start with a small snowball and roll it around the snowy ground until it grows bigger and bigger. The snowflakes on the ground stick to those in the snowball. An avalanche gathers new snow in the same way.

See for Yourself

- Make a snowman. You could use giant snowballs.
- See how long the snowman lasts before it melts.
- Which melts first, the snow lying on the ground or the snowman? Why?
- Why does an icebox take longer to defrost than the rest of the refrigerator?

WINTER SPORTS

Downhill or Alpine skiing is a very exciting sport. Skiers can travel at speeds of more than 200 kilometres per hour. The force of gravity pulls them downwards. To go faster, to steer and to brake, the skiers control the friction of the skis against the snow. This is done by changing the pressure and angle of the skis.

Snowboards are also controlled by friction. The rider has two feet on one board. This allows much greater pressure and **leverage**. The rider can perform acrobatics.

This skier bends right over to reduce the **air resistance**.

In order to balance, the snowboarder has to struggle with the forces of gravity and friction.

The bobsleigh run is smooth, with curved walls of ice. As the bobsleigh corners at high speed, it rises up the wall. This whirling force is called **centrifugal** force.

Riders in toboggans and bobsleighs also use the force of gravity. They control their speed by using friction and pressure too. The riders hunch down so that they create less air resistance. They make a **streamlined** shape.

A bobsleigh team pushes the sleigh off so that it is moving when they jump in. Then their added weight makes the sleigh gather speed quickly.

See for Yourself

See how centrifugal force works:

- Place an ice cube at the bottom of a glass or china mixing bowl.

- Move the bowl repeatedly with a circular motion. What happens to the ice cube?

- Replace the ice cube with a ball of modelling clay. It is not as smooth or hard as the ice cube. What force is slowing the clay down?

WILL THERE BE SNOW?

Farmers, mountain climbers and city councils all need to know if it is going to snow. Farmers have always tried to predict the weather. The clouds gave farmers their best clue. For example, the heavy, low-lying blanket of cloud called **nimbostratus** is very likely to shed snow.

Today, weather forecasts are broadcast on radio and television. The people who prepare forecasts study weather science. They are **meteorologists**.

Weather **satellites** are sent into space to circle the Earth. They send back images of anticyclones and depressions in the **atmosphere** far below. By tracking their progress, meteorologists can forecast snowy conditions.

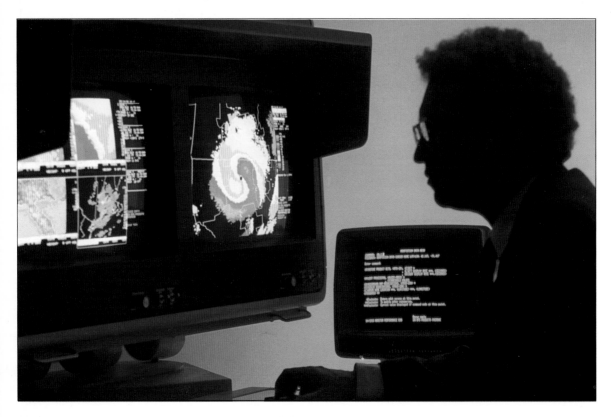

Weather stations all over the world keep records of the weather. Scientists look for general changes in the climate. This meteorological equipment is on board a ship.

Areas of dry weather with few clouds are known as **anticyclones**. They may be bitterly cold, but they produce little snow. Areas of whirling cloud called **depressions** are blown along by the winds. These produce both rain and snow. A tiny difference in temperature can change rain to snow, so forecasting a snowfall can be very difficult.

See for Yourself

Keep a notebook recording weather conditions during a snowy period. Each day:

- Note how cloudy the day is, and how many hours of sunshine there are.
- Buy a cheap outdoor thermometer. Keep a record of the temperature at the same time each day.
- Use a ruler to measure the depth of the snow.
- Note whether the snow is slushy, crisp or powdery.

POLLUTED OR PURE?

Most of the Earth's water (more than 97 per cent) is found in rivers and oceans. Only a small amount (about 2 per cent) is made up of solid ice and snow. The remaining tiny amount is water vapour. Our planet needs pure, fresh water in all these forms in order to work properly. The world's climate, wind patterns and sea levels all depend on the water in the Polar regions.

Human activity has poisoned the air we breathe. The water vapour which makes snow can mix with chemicals, smoke or exhaust fumes from cars to form **acid snow.**

Herds of caribou cross Alaska. They travel under the oil pipelines using underpasses specially made for them. The Arctic **environment** is very fragile. Its wildlife needs protection.

For thousands of years the peoples of the snowy north herded reindeer. But the old way of life is changing. Now people mine, pump oil and build roads in the Arctic. The region is becoming warmer and dirtier.

The world's climate is heating up. This process is called **global warming**. It may be happening because of air **pollution**. Acid snow pollutes northern lakes and forests.

It is time to look after our planet. Many people believe that we should keep Antarctica free from mining and other industries. It is the world's last great wilderness of ice and snow.

The amount of ice around the coasts of Antarctica is becoming less and less each year. It breaks off to form drifting **icebergs**.

WORDS WE USE

absorb	To soak up.
acid snow	Snow which has been polluted by chemicals in the air.
air resistance	The force of air against an object.
anticyclone	A spiral air movement, caused by high pressure.
artificial fibres	Fibres made in a factory, such as nylon.
atmosphere	The layer of gases around a planet.
avalanche	A massive fall of snow down a mountainside.
blizzard	A snowstorm blown by high winds.
centrifugal	Moving outwards from the centre, whirling.
climate	The pattern of weather in one place over a long period.
compass	An instrument used for finding directions. Its needle always points north.
condense	To turn from a gas into a liquid.
crystal	A solid which forms a regular pattern of angled surfaces.
dam	A barrier which prevents the flow of water.
depressions	Air spirals over the Earth's surface, caused by low pressure.
drift	A bank of wind-blown snow.
droplets	Tiny drops. They join to form raindrops, hail or snowflakes.
environment	The world or part of the world around us.
evaporation	The change from liquid into gas.
freezing point	The temperature at which water turns to ice (0°C).
friction	The force which slows one object as it rubs against another.
frost	A covering of ice needles.
frostbite	Damage caused to the skin and flesh by freezing.
gas	An airy substance which fills any space in which it is contained.
global warming	The gradual heating up of our planet.
gravity	The force which pulls objects towards the Earth's surface.
hail	Hard balls of ice that fall like rain.
hydroelectric	Producing electricity from the force of water.
hypothermia	The condition when the body temperature drops to a dangerously low level.

Ice Age	A time when ice spread far from the Polar regions.
iceberg	A large slab of ice which floats through the sea.
insulation	A barrier to keep out heat, electricity or sound.
irrigation	Bringing water to crops in dry lands.
leverage	The power to move something by using pressure.
liquid	A fluid substance, such as water.
meteorologist	A scientist who studies the weather.
nimbostratus	A low, blanket cloud which often produces snow.
Polar regions	The areas around the Earth's most northerly and southerly points.
pollution	The condition where something is poisoned or made impure.
power station	A building where electricity is generated.
refrigerator	A cupboard where goods are cooled electrically, a 'fridge'.
satellite	A spacecraft which is sent up to circle a planet.
settle	To remain frozen after falling on the ground.
ski	A long runner made of wood or other material.
skid	To slip or lose control.
sleet	A mixture of snow and rain.
snow	Precipitation in which water vapour freezes into ice crystals and falls to the ground.
snowflake	A group of ice crystals which stick together and fall to the ground.
solid	A substance which has three dimensions (length, height and width).
streamlined	Having as little wind resistance as possible.
structure	The way in which something is built.
temperature	Warmth or coldness, measured in degrees.
traction	The power a vehicle needs to grip the ground and move forwards.
transhumance	Moving herds between summer and winter pastures.
tread	A pattern of ridges or grooves set in a tyre, to help it grip the road.
turbine	A wheel with blades or vanes which is turned by a gas or liquid.
warm-blooded	Having a warm, constant body temperature.
water cycle	Rain falling, evaporating, rising and condensing in turn, endlessly.
water vapour	A gas created when water evaporates.
weather forecast	An estimate or prediction about future weather conditions.
whiteout	Blizzard conditions in which the human eye sees mostly whiteness.
winched	Wound up on the end of a safety line or cable.

INDEX